God, Do You Understand My Language?
Poetry Collection

Cover Credit: Elle lusk   @ElleryLusk

Table of Contents:

God, Do You Understand My Language?

God, my mother told me,
You are the embodiment of love.
Since then, I have adored you most.
But I wonder do you understand me?
I read your book in the foreign language
of those who rule us.
Are you on the side of missionaries
who pour money into their coffers?
Do you not hear the cry of the children who sleep on dirt floors?
Their souls evaporate into the night
—the dark and cold embrace of death.
How can you ignore
the suffering of a child?
Or the landscape of poverty that swallowed his mother
and misplaced his dad?
He cries in his own language.
Do you understand that language too?
Malnourished mothers 'milk dries in their breast;
They can no longer feed their babies.
Their hands raise to you in despair.
Can't you see, God?
A father who does not beg or steal, starves.
He looks towards you before hanging himself.
I believe you can't be blind to the sight.
Do you greet and welcome his fractured soul?
A poor young girl screamed before being raped
You're not deaf.
Starvation, neglect, illness, and cruelty
are not different in your holy book.
Unless you don't understand
when they're said in my language.
Is the emotion behind them the same,
no matter the place, no matter the people?

Outside a fancy shopping mall,

A little girl sells colorful balloons
to buy medicine for her mother.
She looks towards the sky,
and talks to you.
Do you feel her despair?
A woman on her knees at a corner begs for coins,
a tiny baby in her arms.
In pain, she calls You.
Do her prayers reach You?
Or are they the wrong language?
Do you live in her empty bowl?

Oh God,
We sing hunger songs on holy nights,
high on gospel phrases with a symphony of soul
and faith carrying us down Your path.
We walk the line.
Our arms outstretched toward
the mystic constellations in a crystallin sky.
But You run ahead.
Is our faith only a mantra?

The World is Your creation.
Why won't you listen, almighty savior?
Do You sleep inside a nascent dream?
We ask only for a piece of bread,
no matter if it's stale; we don't care.
We are hungry.
But we receive humiliation and hunger.
I don't dare say
You have a careless heart.
But—could it be true?

Oh, God! Will Your Kingdom never come?
We yearn to walk the road to the edge of the light;
where there is no hunger or death,
where sun does not sting bare skin.
Where intangible, indiscernible

words do not wound us.
Our breath grazes the candle's flame,
at a saint's tombstone.
The flame struggles, in its last moment,
to live or to die.
Are we that candle?
Or smoke dissipating in the darkness?

We were Born to Clap

Dear First World, Salute to you
Accept humble bow, from the Third World.
Thank you for the great lectures for fucking idiots.
Heads hung low, wide-eyed,
we clapped.

You sold us your notion of humanity,
we lived in a barbaric world.
You bombed to end the atrocities.
The boisterous sound of your missiles came over our heads,
we clapped.

You sent us tattered clothes,
and dried milk,
you gifted us stale food.
Wow!
We clapped.

A few of us declined your orders,
and ran to caves,
we saw burnt bones.
Your president called us rats,
We clapped.

You hanged our leaders,
cheered the dictators,
crushed skulls, and scarred souls,
"Surrender and live," your president yelled,
we clapped.

Our women heard the faint screams,
and fell to their knees crying,
their silent prayers stuck between the earth and the sky.
You were the people of God; we the creeping creatures,

we clapped.

We grew up applauding you,
We forgot who we were,
Our heroes bled in silence,
Our haggard faces spoke of fear,
We clapped.

You selected some of us to live in your heaven,
I was one of those who always clapped,
now I was a proud human,
away from the dirt of the Third World,
I clapped.

I met an old man on a shiny pathway,
carrying a box of empty bottles.
He looked at my bottle and said, I sell bottles.
There was loneliness and hunger in his eyes.
I cried.

Love Me from a Distance

Alluring Beauty,
Love me from a distance, for I'm a poet.
Do you know how I squeeze life into words?
I grasp my soul—
to pour your being into a poem
pick up pieces of my broken life.
I walk alone in desolate tracks, a broken shell.
Hiding the smell of death
I eat my demise for lunch
and pour it into a dish for dinner.

Do you know how I create lyrics for you?
I perceive—
to dance with souls of poets
ignored in life and adored in death.
I starve for rhymes at their graves
and search for meanings buried in me.

Do you know what it is to starve?
I feel—
to chase a bluebird
with crippled fingers ; and clouds for vision
shimmering feathers dulled to teal smudges.
I cry at night, bowed before my muse's feet
silent screams ripping the sky.
The ethereal bird laughs and sings
Go enjoy your constipated world.

I'm man-bitten
there is no Helen of Troy in my poisoned life
I walk on the fire.
For paltry sums I signed a contract with Lucifer,
starting with damnation and no "Consummatum est."
You would be misplaced in my private whirlwind

I don't want to lose you.
So, save your flowers.

Come when I'm in grave;
I'll rise up to kiss you.

The Laughter of a Call Girl

Walking along the town street,
hand in hand with loneliness.
The moon flashed through leaves and highlighted a call girl
standing hipshot at a bus stop.

Her beauty touted open desire,
I smiled and sidled her,
"I want to write a poem about you,
You, the wild girl of the city."

Transfixed by a pale orb,
she spoke these haunting words.
"My existence is amber
Poems can't express my being.
It is a dark void I swim in.
My soul resides in a dark place.
My skies are tainted black.
There are no rainbows.

My skin is a neon welcome sign;
It flashes artificial yellow, green then blue.
an invitation for rough hands
and dirty words to follow me.

I am the sidewalk beneath trampling feet,
crunching and cracking under their weight.
My life exists between legs –
a delicate meat.
The hungry vultures circle above
with sharp beaks and talons to tear
what's left of me.

This suffocating city, these thousands of people
can't see with eyes washed clean.
Walking over skeletons with hardened hearts,

their eyes burrow through my clothing,
imagining their filthy pleasures.
They come to get me,
Pushing me into shadows
where they all belong—
lifeless, still, dead and empty,
Oh, these wooing slaves, pretending to be masters!"

She paused as if to say more, but her bus pulled in.
Apologizing, she shook her head,
"I can't miss the bus for a poet."
Yet, one favor she left me.
Before leaving,
she looked back, and guffawed.
The piano jangled away at the nearby bar.

Her laughter now wanders with me in the streets,
full of fears, mockery, blame, guilt and questions.
"Oh, you city of 'civilized' people,
Wear a brave face and don't hide from the cracks."

The UN Rides on Human Skeletons

The UN's representatives
Suited in beautiful attire
Torchbearers of justice
Warriors against poverty
They strut before cameras
Magic bags in hands,
Walking, heads bowed
Carrying weight of the planet.

They ponder destiny of the bleeding earth
Sitting on cozy chairs
The Secretary General pushes peace
Promising of better days.

Far from the cameras
Missing limbs
Pay the Cost of War
Leaving behind hungry orphaned children
Suffering unending grief.

In the name of patriotism
Young soldiers, torn from family
Their eyes like kittens
Separated from mother
They sleep in ditches dug in mud
They kill the enemy during the day
And see the dead, dancing and laughing at night.
Guilt cripples them more than battle
In the loneliness these "brave" men
Curse the curses their generals spat at the enemy.

Peace
This promise rides on human skeletons
So absurd, amid a stretch of war.

Eight-year old Olena lies in a Ukraine hospital
The sun colors her dolls
Left in a broken pieces of home
Her burnt body, an unread page of her cut-short life
What worth is the UNO to her?
She never chanced at hello
Could only say goodbye.

News cameras in Afghanistan,
An old man rasping with languid lungs
Buries his young son
Wiped-Out
Because he was a singer
UNO charter sings
Peace, dignity, and equality
On a healthy planet.

The blue wrecked ship sinks
Peace mocks through shattered spars
Sleeping on flowery mats
The Security Council dreams
Another amazing sermon
Preaching peace to the world-wide family
Discovering love in human DNA.

My Hometown

My hometown, my lost friend,
Thank you for greeting me once again,
at a time when we both are lost.
When I wander your streets,
you also wander within me,
weaved into my thoughts.
Winding down to your core,
to the oldest part of you,
I finally remember your last hug.
Let's hug once again to soothe sorrows.

I left you in chase of dreams,
but the silence of your smooth brick walls
always called me back, haunting me to recall my origin.
Do you remember when I climbed up your bosom?
Swept up to your canals on the rustle of your voice in the wind?
I remember cycling up streets of yours,
through rows of antiquated shops,
the vast green fields coming into view.

I stretched on your arms and legs to the sand hills,
where your voice blew fainter than a whisper.
Your vast cemetery is a reminder of where we stand in relation.
And how in death, you hold us tight against your bosom still.
I know that your greens and parks are like your dreams.
And your slums, your plazas, are your nightmares.
How granite manors, dilapidated ruins of industry,
slums, and cafes dot your skin harmoniously.

Now I glance your history over thick stone railings.
Modernity to your face makes you sad,
an unclouded glimpses of your ancient face cries,
and I'm here to wipe your tears.
Your hug brings back my pleasures.
Some are darkened subconscious – like late nights walks,
embedded in drunken haze, winding to romanticism of my youth.

Others are gracefully vivid, the walks through the mango gardens,
holding my father's hand, and dreaming of unknown world
Now extend your hand to remember that lost hand.

Winding down to your core, to the oldest part of you,
I finally remember your name.
It rolls off my tongue like the sound plucked strings off a harp.
It is there that I know who you were.
It is then that your message –
– brings me peace in its clarity once more.
You are like the rediscovery of an old photograph –
bringing me peace in its clarity once more.
You are the city that made me,
and to who I owe my fondest memories.

Heed that I am older now,
I walk a shorter pace and sleep a longer hour.
Beautiful women in spring, in the sun,
only bring nostalgic sorrow to my heart,
I long to find you one last time,
My hometown, my lost friend.

A Love Letter to Pandemic

Blinking at the shift schedule,
I sparkled in the days of Covid.
As a doorman, I stood firm for eight hours.
My nightmares dragged me six feet under.
Winter hugged me tight still I thrived.
My employer waved at me from behind glass,
and sent appreciation letters.
"You're a real hero;
We salute your bravery."
I wanted to shout:
"I'm hungry not brave.
My hunger is vicious,
more powerful than a million Covid germs."

Today I was laid off,
And Covid whispered
"Bye for now,
"You're a failure."
Mocking the echoes of "hero"
I implored in return:
"My benefactor, my livelihood,
I love your protracted pandemic chill,
Please come back.
I starve again."

I Vomit Poems

I'm a modern poet.
Pyromaniac.
Psychotic.
And schizophrenic.

Living in emptiness,
I walk in the convolutions of absurdity.
Idiocy spreads over me like the sky.
My poetry storms between cozy shelters and rocky waves,
while the world rushes toward suicide.
Suffocated, I lift my head
but I'm dragged down by viscous triviality.

My tongue is burned
with the acid of loathing
I gawk at the world.
Crawling through the madness,
I welcome the garb of another day.
My life measured by pale, gray days.
A stray dog at a butcher's shop
that stays all the day without chains,
and yowls others for leftovers.

I learned to worship agony.
I'm a commodity made in a cheap factory,
an item in a grocery list.
My heart a broken shell.
I don't write; I vomit poems.

The Last Message of a Hanged Leader

My dreams scare you ~~~~
your loathing anguish is my glory.
You put me in a gutter
of your gnarly mediocrity
I still enjoy the sky ~~~
And watch you shudder.

Why do you rush past me?
Wait!
Let your sting be more lethal.
Enjoy my stumbling in the land of ignorance.
Allow flocks of vultures to circle over me.
let the world see you
dancing in the flames of my soul!
Wait for the crows to come
and peck my soul.
You watch my agony
while I gather my scattered dreams.

Don't think me a blank canvas
and paint as you please.
with a brush dipped in your vat of dirty thoughts.
The horrors of your ugly mind don't touch
the ocean of love I hold.
The rhythm of my persona echoes
in distant meadows of lonely souls,
walking through a forgotten garden of broken hearts.
And you're just holding tale of White Elephant,
that will piss on your face, when I'm gone.

You killed and threw me into your river of hatred,
and thought I was consumed.
You hung my head by your sting,
but my soul clawed for the surface, gasped for air,
sank and then rose breathing anew.

Now I'm everywhere in the hearts of people.
I'm a shadow hugging a tired tree,
a cool evening wind whispering to the thirsty leaves,
I'm the lullaby of prismatic rivers and sweeping hills
that runs to dying fields, and frozen lakes.
Nature sneers at you:
"Here comes my child, so untamed, wild, and free."

You were the Moon

One morning a beautiful purple flower,
bloomed in the burning desert,
where the scorching sun holds sway.
Baked by the deadly heat,
yet still it blossomed,
held its head high,
and shouted, Bravo!
Burning rays bleached it, yet it never wilted.
Thirst turned its petals yellow; but it kept striving.
The pride of desiccated leaves made the desert furious.
The relentless sun flared at it.
The wind threw fits of temper,
And battered this flower endlessly,
With sandstorm that choked out its air.
It bent for a while,
then raised again.
The furious sun came over its head,
determined to kill it.
A wild and hungry bird,
pecked at the dying petals.
But the flower kept its pride,
The angry sun stained its lips red
yet its feeble, wounded leaves danced on.

Crushed by the humble evening,
the arrogant sun's last rays died
at the roots of flower.
The arrogant sun sounded like a void,
collapsed lungs, leaving only
the silence of its grimace.
When the cool of twilight came,
to heal the wounds
the flower opened its heart to give fragrance,
to the lifeless desert.

The moon came with its cool light.

Vanity of the Sun took its last breath
in a soft silver sand.
White beams hugged the flower,
it rose again as if it had never suffered.
Desert's scorching yellow sand,
turned cool when dark shadow
kissed the tips of her toes.

The moon and flower sang a folk song,
that infused the yellow sand,
and lulled the tired caravans.
When the desert slept,
the moonlight in the sky lit up its soul.
to warm a tired heart,
the moon glow bruised the red lips.
The moon and the flower hugged,
shared other one's kiss and divine secrets.

Nature flourished in that moment.
The silence of the desert spoke,
the language of memory,
of rapturous light and fragrance.
The gentle wind stole the white illuminating dreams,
and went away to touch the hearts of poets.

You were the moon, I the flower.

Your Touch

Through the window of my room,
I behold the white mountains,
the sunlight beams down,
reflecting back on me.
My soul merges with the colors.
In the twilight of your beautiful city,
a lonely bird disappears in the horizon.
I feel you.

The rain starts in the hot desert,
the thirsty sand smiles.
I lay on the cool wet land,
you become my landscape,
I feel you.

But I have to be among humans;
they surround me like hungry growling hyenas,
I'm a deer trying to escape:
they close in on me,
tear my soul apart,
kick my suffering essence
like the winning team kicks the victory ball;
pieces of my being scatter in the air,
the vultures come and attack me with sharp beaks.
In the full moonlight.
the cries of my soul
shake the far skies.
I miss you.

And then you come,
gather the pieces of my soul,
clean the bleeding wounds.
Blessed in your hands,
I feel marvelous again.
Soaring to the dancing stars,
I feel you.

Your Love was a Firefly

As a child I dreamt of chasing fireflies.

Watching them hover over shadowy valleys,

like diamond sparkling over the fields

singing pastoral songs throughout the endless night,

glowing with the blue light,

a dancing rainbow for the eyes innocent,

sending a wink to the moon.

I caught one when I was five.

Crushed it tight, not to lose it.

The little bug tickled my palm,

flamed out like shining from shook foil

and then it ceased to be.

Light yet composed, with a lingering soft stare, I cried:

"Grandpa, life and light both gone."

He hugged me close:

"Behold their joyous dance.

But don't touch their spirit."

Years later I found you, love.

Grandpa's advice, long forgotten.

the light of love in your eyes drew me.

I gravitated to your embrace,

to find another corpse,

not in my palm, but in my heart.

The symphony of your voice lost

to a cacophony of crickets.

each dream lingering after dawn.

telling me the truth I don't want to hear,

strangling a once thriving beauty.

Neither childhood nor the valley,

my heart longs for the dead firefly.

Love's Death Anniversary

You didn't attend our love's funeral.
Do you even remember the life we shared?
What you killed in its youth.

It's the anniversary of our love's
death.
So celebrate together.

Throw new soil on the grave,
cover it with stones,
and mark the grave "Love is Contagious".

Victims of love lose their rationale,
wander in the barren fields,
as their sighs surround around them.

let's save the world from the wound of love,
rescue our generation by stoning it,
Your world is known for stones, bring the hardest.

let's dig another grave for them,
all those books that bred love between us,
and bury our disease.

How cheerful was our love!
Its glory rivaled the most vibrant of flowers,
it once flew and brought crystal beams,

Though our love enlightened our souls,
it vanished when you threw love down a dark well,
Where it cried for many nights.

I pulled up the love you cast away.
There will be no time to bury it deeper,
never forget the day our love died.

Your Footprints on Snow

Since you left,
sorrow dances on the white streets,
Love is a drum,
beating with sad hands,
The drum cries like a lost child
birds forget their songs,
people, like dogs, cower.
You draped old dreams
on naked trees.
Nightingales devoured those dreams
and became ghosts,
on white mountains.

You walked on snow,
long strides, head held high, away from me.
trailing footprints that tell the story,
you wrote while pausing to push
your knife in my heart.
Perhaps to hear the cries of my soul.

I hurried to get closer to you,
Only your footprints on the snow,
I chased until,
They grew wings and left.
I couldn't fly like you,
You took my wings,
my sighs linger in sad air.

I thought I saw hope in the space between your footprints
I wish you would come back.
Every year snow falls,
burying your footprints,
in a deeper graveyard
of my heart, unseen by the world.

I Carry the Burden of Dreams

I wish I could lead you back to the weaving tracks,
we carved in our youth
the white mare we rode together,
I cupped hands and heaved you up
picked the mushrooms,
and above all, the dreams we shared.

Listen: those dreams are heavier now,
I can't carry them by myself.
I wonder if you'd remember, the way I do,
The dreams you helped create.
Remember that one dream?
The one kissing in the moonlight?
Last night, the moon and I wept for that.

Our dreams have become so old,
and don't let me sleep
my heart cramps when I weep for our dreams.
I touch them alive again!

You told me you would hear my cries at night.
Would you now listen to the creak of my bones
as they protest every bend?
People say I'm old~
the mirror sees not wrinkles on my face,
caused by the weight of long, aged dreams
that drag me to my knees.

Do they not still call to you?
They seek you in dark alleys.
Come back and take your dreams,
I can't carry them alone.

How Should I forget you?

I wake up every day, promising myself to forget,
yet I always find myself wandering back to Y.O.U
your love is as fresh as the morning dew.
Rays of sunlight kiss my face
reminding me of your lips
as we sucked in the cold morning air
and created our small intimate universe.
Your love arches like a transparent rainbow
and ours sparks burst into colors.

The sun passes over its high noon perch
and I sit down for lunch convincing myself that now
I really must forget you,
but the sun warms me like you would
as our skin danced to the music of your moaning
and your body's sensual warmth
providing me heavenly pleasures
delights as promised by :God.

Now, the sun is deep in the horizon
and my mood is as somber as the day you left
I vow once again to forget you,
but the sun's light fades like you walking away
reminding me of your unexpected departure
and our LOST joys.
The dooming sun is like that corner of the road
where you turned left, hidden from my longing gaze
the sun retreated towards the darker corners of the sky.
My desire to forget you dissipates with the dark
the ink-BLACK –NIGHT encompasses everything
so out of my fear of a dark heart in the dark night
I talk to your shadow:
Your shining love cradles me — the cupids singing
— -the praise of your bright eyes
their song rises beyond the skies
waking up the sleeping gods
as I fall A-sleep.

In my dream I meet the lonely God
Hugging me tight, he whispers:

“I created this world out of love
My desire permeates your realm.”

First Love's Memory

After a long hot summer,
today a light wind cools my skin,
reminding me of you.
caressing my soul.
I think of our first embrace,
the taste of your kiss lingers,
and your memory lulls my heart.
The coolness of your touch,
shivers to bitter cold,
hardens to ice within my soul.
I'm alone,
since you walked away.

Many years ago,
my youth satisfied your hunger,
and the longing for love in my soul,
yet, a forever young soul surpasses,
love lust's passions.
My first love's memory soothes my aching heart.
But, for your hunger now,
what comforts your ache now, my love?

Farewell Song for Migrating Cranes

Farewell migrating cranes,
your fields have turned dry,
like the heart of my country--a long journey awaits.
Although it may kill,
yet you rip through the air with certainty and grace.
Let me wave,
and listen to your song one last time,
your holy hymns to the choir.
You will find your green fields,
but I've lost mine forever.

I wish for a song,
that could soothe the harsh climate,
and melt the white mountains,
but my poetic vision is narrow,
and can't reach the god of weathers,
it withers on the bough,
I wish it could capture the holy spirit,
and my soul could soar light as you,
but sitting alone I ponder,
what would this ghost-like land will show me,
without you.

Goodbye dear departing friends,
Are you flying in pain?
In agony of your departure?
Some of you were born here,
and now you go to an unknown world,
unaware of the hunters,
who are loading guns for you.
You who will fly hundreds of miles,
Only to be welcomed by bullets.

Oh, my friends, I can relate,
I came to your land as an immigrant,
in the days of sorrow and sadness,
your songs gave me hope,
your sweet melodies,
savored moments of joy,
you told me how to survive in strange lands,
and now you are leaving me alone.

I want to fly with you,
away from the world of humans,
where hatred spreads like drifting snow,
that has not melted for centuries.

Oh, old crane,
I want to see you lead your flock,
towards the warm lands,
where you teach about life,
our leaders have left us to the harsh winds.
I envy your free flights,
Your brave songs make me strong,
As you flit,
red leaves fall on the ground
from the amber sky you look down.

If you can't stay anymore,
take my heart with you,
carry into the vast skies,
where it will have peace,
away from the dirt of the human world.
I know it has become heavier,
by the weight of centuries,
it contains the tears of mothers,
whose sons never returned.
Sorrow of migration bleeds my heart,
it has witnessed the human cruelty,
and above all the pain of lost love.

Carry my love with you,
and lose it in the open seas,
Where the blue water will purify it,
and green islands will embrace it.
Let it dwell there for a few months,
and if you come back,
bring it with you,
to loft again,
forever high.

A Void, We Call Life

When words fall short,

I sit in the world's shadows.

Watching the world through my window,

I rejoice absurd songs.

Life spills in laissez faire economics,

consuming dreams to rust.

Forgotten blue and white banners flutter.

Wind sighs in Red Oaks,

echoing the doleful cries of a lonesome.

The song rises:

a kite lifted by a gust

of ethereal wind.

Through my window,

humans look like pieces of unknown debris.

Scattered and strewn without rhyme nor reason,

Withered leaves swish through the grass,

Dandelions soar through the air

Rain falls like the tears of a homeless boy,

while a little girl sings::

"The Lord is taking a bath today."

A street sweeper laughs:

"Now I understand why God is cold."

Migratory birds fly by,

their eyes to the skies.

Angry crows peck the snow.

A duck walks towards the edge of a frozen lake,

staring at the surface.
A lyrebird cries from a bed of reeds.
Who am I to judge them?
I am no savior or hostage.
But merely human corruption, tattooed with invisible ink
on pages of The New York Times that keep me warm.
I'm forced up against a window,
I peer through refracted lenses.

I envy those people who finished themselves.
They didn't desire heaven or fear hell.
Imagining nothingness,
they jumped to taste the bottom.
Fear of the unknown keeps me alive in this void,
we call life.
I open the window
and watch as life goes by
like a bat's dream.

My Merciless Muse

Oh, merciless muse.
Break your silence. Unveil your face.
Loose your lips,
wave your wisp of hair from your eyes.
teach me how to compose lyrics from my heart.

I've much to sing.
Many tunes wait uncelebrated.
Verses wither before birth.
Lyrics slip away unsung,
like leaves in a gale.
The dry poetry in my soul rests like Ezekiel's bones.

You told me a long time ago:
Bathe in the beauty of life,
immerse yourself in its allure.
I tried to follow your words.
And took a drive to the sea.
Life bloomed around me as I dove,
But when I found the ocean,
my thoughts returned to sorrow.
The trip crucified me.
Yet, you remained silent.

I sip the wine of love,
lost in sight of sorrows.
However the booze too, remained fruitless.

Love tortured me,
Love lost and lust glistened,
Still, you were indifferent.

Come, let's talk!
Be my heart.
Be my breath.
Be my whole self.
Tighten your grip around me,
my heart longs for unrequited love.
Let it coil around my being
like the sweet wine of Russia.
Set my heart ablaze.
Allow me to write,
words never written ever.
Lay down with me
at the shores of poesies.
Your immortal kiss will nourish my words
and breathe life into my poetry.
Fill the void with all your might,
and let me sing my song,
until it echoes across the universe.

Have You Stopped Hating Me?

The sun no longer burns me
The clouds hugged away the moon last night
The stars sang from behind the curtain
Have you stopped hating me?

The cuckoo returns to the garden
as flowers sway in the breeze
and the nightingale dances on my patio wall.
Have you stopped hating me?

The storms go unreported.
The torrents of rain disappear.
And in the still night, the wolf howls are not heard.
Have you stopped hating me?

There's no more horror in the waves of the sea
The earth no longer shakes
Even the graveyard dogs are silent
Have you stopped hating me?

Oh God, Give Twist to Life's Drama

To get rid of your monotony, Dear God,
You wrote a play.
But Your characters forgot their lines,
and mere noise comes from the stage.
While Darkness pervades across the land,
Your actors growl and snarl.
Goodness evaporates.
In disgust, You behold humans' phony sanctimony,
savoring the stench of rotting flesh.
The wolf chasing the old elk,
boasts about hunts of death.
I see You weeping at Your clowns
Your script leaks, dripping barren circles of ash.

Oh God, give this play a twist.
Come, immerse yourself in life's drama.
Repair what our shrieking souls have done,
haunted by a loss of purpose.
Lists of empty words scrawled across loose-leaf notebooks
We creep around Your window,
vomiting filth on your beautiful world.
Change this absurd play.
Tears and shame fill our eyes.
Broken hearts.
Shattered souls.
What can be more befitting a human?
In Your galaxies of love and wonder,

don't search for lost human soul.

Oh God, reveal a new Act,

Or, draw the curtain.

Hammer Your Words

Hey, Baby.
Don't suppress your hatred.
Open your thesaurus
and find all nasty words for me
Mouth off, trash-talk me,
and I promise to change them into a song
the future generations will use our song
in their love letters.
I'm a poet,
with the magic to change
the meanings of words.
Hammer your words,
and see how my touch makes them mild and tender.
I bleed but never cry.
Yet, I exist within your words — an unhealed wound.
My kisses are petals.
So, speak up, don't hide.
Look right into my eyes!
I'll pack your vicious punch
in a bouquet of love
I, who can snatch life
from the claws of death.

A Common Man's Love Story

I'm a commoner
fighting the demons of bills, of food, of life.
My meager pension enough to buy
slippers and a jacket at a thrift store.
Once, I sought stars
Now
I hide behind a trashcan of dreams.
I am a statistic,
known only by my photo ID.
A bomb blasts and news channels read:
Another sixty or so,
dead.
Death pauses eating
but soon resumes her feast.
I am a number on her dining table.
I have no place for pride,
crawling for crumbs of life
with mangled hands.

Years ago
as I stepped through white moaning snow,
I met a pretty girl
taking shelter for a bus
like a freshly feathered bird
Her hazel eyes flicked towards mine.
Snagged for a moment —
ice on a stove.

We loved in blessed silence
She, a promised paradise.
But pledges faded
like colors of rainbow:
purple, blue, yellow, and colors never seen.
I slept there for a while,
and awoke to wind's sad song
birds mourning
cold reality tugging my naked dreams.

Many years later
We met again under that shelter
She with her children
Me with mine.
She held mortgage papers
I clutched my rent receipts
We did not speak
but smiled at how rotten fate
spread over our lives
a poor sketch of a tombstone —
cemetery hidden under cypress trees.
We lived between heaven and hell.
Where once, we jumped in a sea of life
and fell into commonness' jaw.

Stuck in the panes of sky
I wait for God to open His door,
and reply to my hungry prayers.

Do Not Growl

You cast me to demons.
I suffer beneath their teeth.
Their jaws clenched tight,
around my throat, around my heart.

Do not growl at my fall.
Do not howl at the moon.

I'm lost in the abyss,
but re-born dreams fill my heart.
Someone awaits there
— my true self, lured by hope.
like a phoenix, I will be reborn

Do you see ripples kissing the shore?
That is me.
I know how trees grow on rocks.
I am a seedling sprouting from the pavement.
You will see me floating like indigo butterflies.
You will feel me as the breeze that breezes your eyes.
You will smell me in the honeysuckle blossom.

Love You Still, Pakistan

O, Pakistan, where should I begin?
A British stronghold, a century of colonial rule,
that relegated us to clowns.
Now we're neither British nor Asian.
Ridiculous, a half-way between nowhere.
Our mother tongue called to us, her words broken.
This voice that once withstood the oppression of daggers.
Our culture, self-depreciated.
We became illusions behind allusions.
a nation-state born of crises
Independence serendipitous—
a designed divorce from our neighbor.
Our shouted victories and cries of defeat,
comprehended by neither side.
Bullets drew forth blood, but never achieved a win.
Rhetoric textbooks make-up we're compelled to wear
Our history was written in blood.
Our poor parallel structure line to line.
We bought weapons with gold we did not have.
And poverty rules our streets.
Famine dances, her nakedness mocks us.
We go to mosques but seek salvation from financiers
As if the IMF could quell fear.
We are forced to elect a better beggar,
which perpetuates suffering to spread for our umpteenth generation.

O, Pakistan how do I convey?
I hate the patriotism
invented to hide dirt,
and expose others spoilage.
Through excruciating lessons, you taught me about failure.
Now when someone asks about you,
I tell them about mangoes and oranges.
But not the rapes of peasant girls,
behind the delicious fruit trees.

O, Pakistan, I survive in silence.
Justice imprisoned in the court buildings and barracks.
By whom shall it be unchained?
A myriad of policies govern our lives,
while silver tongues line gunmen's pockets.
I've heard enough of being a corrupt state,
—a third world democracy.
We love military parades but hate cultural activities,
reduced to a nation of sterile, unthinking people,
who live the mistruths spouted by the academics.

O, Pakistan, how should I forget Gawadar Bay Sands?
Where over the abyss our wealth spills.
But in return you tell the stories of the missing youth.
The subtle, insidious ways to jail and exile activists, and
grandmothers who wash dead bodies of their grandchildren.

O, Pakistan, how do I speak of thee?
Your liberal media broadcasts don't care about food,
bleeding stories, and colloquial ways.
The tenacity of our ancestors fleeing wounded countries,
or the stubborn fighting spirit that never bows,
bustling crowds at the Sunday Bazar.
I grew up in your sun-struck land,
every vein, wrinkle, blood vessel
harshly branded into my heart.
You were a beautiful beloved
who flirted with a means to an end.
Your memory is like the stories of Manto,
and poems of Charles Bukowski.
Despite your aging spirit reeking of greed, vitriol and oppression,
I love you.

Dead Leaves

Uptown.
Downtown.
All around.
Swirls of people
Touched by the kiss of absurdity.
Flesh creating more flesh.
A city grown in tumor ridden tentacles.
Jumbled steel, glass, concrete and asphalt
Built up in rows of skyscrapers.
Whose long, jagged teeth bite holes through the heavens.
Streets flow with cars and people
Like rivers bent into sharp angles.
Bulging subway vehicles,
Merge from the city's cold metallic underbelly.
A woman, dwarfed by giant towers,
paces a bridge,
Her shoulders bent with the burden of nit-picked dreams.
She bites a lip as winter nips her cheeks.
Humming low and anxious,
Purse clutched to her chest,
She's lost youth, beauty and happiness to the ravages of time.
The sour pavement beneath her feet does not care.
Nor does the world.
The stars are deaf to her fretful tune.
The woman gazes the indifferent moon between the clouds,
And knows it does not care either.
Her eyes see the years of her past.
And she becomes an unnoticed splash in the river
A fish jumps near as ripples fade along the surface.
Blackout.
Quiet water lulls her desires.
She is no longer present.
The stars move on.
Death thirsts for blood anew.
People continue to swirl.
Dead leaves that scurry in circles.